W9-BIN-497

SANTA CRUZ
DEL
VALLE DE LOS CAIDOS

SANTA CRUZ

DEL

VALLE DE LOS CAIDOS

MADRID
EDITORIAL PATRIMONIO NACIONAL
1984

All rights reserved «Patrimonio Nacional»
Plaza de Oriente - 28013 Madrid
PRINTED BY FISA - BARCELONA
Legal Deposit B. 34069-1984
ISBN 84-7120-051-1

CONTENTS

THE Monument of the Holy Cross of the Valley of the Fallen stands in the parish of San Lorenzo del Escorial. It covers an area of 1,365 hectares, bounded on the North by the parish of Guadarrama, and on the South by the stream of Guatel, the Solana estate, and the Hill of Jurisdiction. To the East runs the highroad from the Escorial to Guadarrama and the Solana, and to the West lie the parishes of Peguerinos and Santa María de la Alameda. It is from 985 and 1,758 metres above sea level, its highest point being El Risco de los Abantos.

It is 58 kms. from Madrid, 55 from Avila and 45 from Segovia. From Madrid it is reached by the Coruña highroad. A fine Autobahn leads to Las Rozas, where it divides on the left to the Escorial and on the right to Segovia by the Lion's Pass. The whole landscape is typical of Velázquez.

On the way to the Lion's Pass, a little before the town of Guadarrama (50 kms. from Madrid) and after going across the bridge over the River of the same name, if we keep on to the left, along the Escorial road, we come to the entrance to the valley, about 8 kms. further on. The grandeur of the monument and its buildings catch the eye at once. A romantic, rocky valley opens out before us. The only vegetation consists of pines, broom, oaks, ebony trees and poplars, just a few of the latter in a sheltered corner. There are also some holm-oaks and holly, together with brambles, thyme, marjoram and other aromatic herbs, which give an austerity to the landscape befitting the proximity of the Guadarrama Mountains. At the top of a rocky gorge the Risco de la Nava rises high and remote, a cone-shaped crag of bare rock surrounded on three sides by mountains overshadowed in their turn by the peaks of Navacerrada. On the open side, facing East, lies the wide valley in all tis grandiose beauty.

The previous Head of State conceived the monument and chose the site for it.

A decree issued on April 1st 1940 ordered the monument to be erected, and don Pedro Muguruza Otaño, Director General of Architecture and the leading Spanish architect at that time, was entrusted with the task of carrying out the plans.

Work was soon started on the present Hospice and Centre of Studies, and the hollowing out of the Crypt in the mountainside began. Geological surveys were made as well as research into the climactic conditions of the site; contracts were competed for, plans offered, and designs drawn up for the layout. The famous architect entrusted with the inmense task fell ill in 1948 and was unable to finish it, so that finally, after some attempts at technical collaboration, don Diego Méndez González was asked to carry on.

Ten years had gone by, and still the two most important parts of the monument had not been erected: the Crypt and the Cross. The Basilica was indeed the core of the design, and this had to be built right inside the mountain called El Risco de la Nava. The hollowing out of its interior already achieved would have to be considerably greater, to comply with the grandiose scale of the plans. The tunnel measured 11 × 11 metres, and its dimensions were adhered to for the entrances to the great aisle, which measures double its height, 22 metres. The new architects started the enlargement of the Crypt fully aware of the difficulties involved. Chief among these was the placing of the immense Cross, embedded in tons of concrete and granite, upon the hollow mountain.

It will therefore be understood that a work on this scale could not be carried out in a hurry. Diego Méndez was able, however, to overcome the many difficulties arising from its singular situation and imaginative scope, as can be seen today in the finished monument.

The present Residence was completed in November 1950, and the erection of the Cross was approved, work upon it starting in 1951; the great esplanade was planned in 1952 and the enlargement of the Crypt approved. Work on this lasted throughout 1953 and 1954, when the transept was planned. In 1955, the stone facings to the walls and dome of the Crypt, the galleries and Vestry

were begun. In 1956, the choir, altars and paving of the
Crypt were built, and lastly in 1957, the rear portico and
the great cloister. The Monastery and Novices' Residence
were begun, and completed in 1958.

The numerous and varied problems of a practical, esthe-
tic, expressive and imaginative nature were solved, and
the inmense Cross on the mountain-top, and the vast
church within, at last took shape.

Entrance to the Valley. The Juanelos.

Once inside the Valley, a wide road takes us up to the
Monument itself. A few metres from the entrance, to
right and left of the road, stand the monolithic shafts
known as The Juanelos. They were quarried at Fonseca
and Nambroca and carved in the sixteenth century for
the use of the famous Juanelo Turriano. They now stand
like sentinels guarding the way into the Valley

A lofty viaduct levels the road and well-planned ramps
take us up to the causeway going up to the esplanade and
the Crypt, the Monastery, Hospice and Centre of Social
Studies, Via Crucis and the great Cross crowning the
Valley.

The Causeway and Esplanade.

A magnificent stairway, 100 metres wide, leads up from the road. It is in two flights, of ten steps each, symbolizing the Ten Commandments, or the ascent to moral perfection inspired by faith. It is hewn out of the live rock and ends in the great esplanade of 30,600 square metres. It is paved in the shape of a cross, the corners filled in with crazy paving whose crevices are sown with clover and ryegrass. A wide, stout parapet surrounds the centre part of the esplanade, separating it from the two sides which are reached by flights of granite steps.

Another stairway of fifteen steps, 63 metres wide, leads to the door of the Crypt flanked by two classic arcades.

The Great Cross.

The Cross is the predominating feature of the whole monument. It rises to command the Valley and excite the admiration of all beholders. Its beauty of line, its proportions strictly related to the size of the mountain, the way it springs out of the fine rocky crest of the massive Risco de la Nava, and the elegance of its outline against the sky, all combine to give it aesthetic as well as symbolic value. Added to this is the realization of technical difficulties overcome in its construction by its architect, Diego Méndez.

The Cross consists of three principle parts: a solid base upon which stand the figures of the four Evangelists; surmounted by a smaller base from which the shaft rises, and at whose four corners are placed the figures of the Four Cardinal Virtues. Above this rises the Cross itself. The first base is 25 metres high, the second 42, while the Cross soars to a height of 150 metres from its base and stands 300 metres above the esplanade, measured from the entrance to the Crypt.

It is formed by a series of oblong prisms which make a Greek Cross, with raised sections in soft relief that take away the starkness of a flat Cross in two prisms. After this dimensional aspect of the Cross, we come to the greatest problem of all; its elevation. It was planned from within like a factory chimney, thus simplifying the haulage of building materials by the longitudinal hollowing-out of the mountain from the rear, until it was joined to the vertical base of the Cross. A lift was installed to lift the huge stones, and to avoid the risks and damage to the mountain produced by works on this vast scale.

Once the shaft of the Cross had been built there were no more difficulties until the cross-bar was reached. The arms, 46 metres in length, were wide enough inside for two average-sized motorcars to pass each other.

The Sculpture at the base
of the Cross

Sculpture of a special kind was needed by the architect to complete the Cross. The original plan was to include the Twelve Apostles, but the number was finally reduced to the four Evangelists at the base itself, and the four Cardinal Virtues at the smaller base from which the shaft springs. This was conceived as the only transition possible from the crest of the mountain itself to the pure lines of the shaft and arms of the Cross.

Just as the architectural difficuties arose from the colossal size of the Cross, the sculptural problems were the outcome of the immense dimensions of the figures and the placing of the granite blocks forming each group. Normal canons vanish before their might and volume, combined with the fantastic proportions of the rocks themselves. Only a deep understanding of the part played by nature in the making of the monument, together with a sense of the tortured flame-like quality of the crags of El Risco, could succeed in creating harmony, through sculpture, between rock and Cross.

Looking up at the Cross from its base, we see how architecture has allied itself to nature by both utilizing and serving her at the same time, and that the sculpture of Juan de Avalos has done the same. His groups of figures have all the rugged strength the site demands. The figure of St. John, leaning forward, seems on the point of hurling itself through the air. St. Luke sits astride the bull with upraised head, St. Mark swings vigorously round on the back of his lion, while St. Mateo reads from an enormous book. All these figures are at one with the rocks themselves, and are all the same blackish hue.

Each Evangelist is 18 yarde high, the average height of a six-storey house. These groups of sculpture weigh 20,000 tons, which, added to the 181,740 tons of the Cross, make a total of 201,740 tons.

The Basilica. The Doorway

The Doorway is composed of two Norman arches with rusticated interiors, in a simple design of oblongs.

The bronze door is the work of the sculptor Fernando Cruz Solís. It measures 10.40 by 5.80 metres and is decorated with panels in relief depicting the fifteen mysteries of the Rosary: while texts from the Apostles are illustrated along the lower frieze. These scenes, treated with the severe elegance of great Spanish religious sculpture, give proof of the artist's quality and his knowledge of modern smelting processes.

The doorway is crowned by a sculptured group of figures representing the Pieta, the work of Juan de Avalos, author of the statuary at the base of the Cross.

The recumbent form of the Saviour, his head slightly raised by his Holy Mother, who gazes with infinite sadness at her Son's face, is seen against the bare background of the Valley, which adds to the beauty of the group.

The outer emplacement of the scene, so near the spot where the Cross rises from the mountain-top, the stark simplicity of the figures, their immense size, together with the colour of the stone, is enough to stir the emotions of even the most hardened unbeliever.

The close collaboration between architect and sculptor is clearly made manifest, and the simplicity of the doorway makes a generous tribute to the artistic beauty of the statuary. Carved in black Calatorao stone, the group measures 12 metres long and 5 metres high.

The Crypt.

The Crypt represents the sum total of all the difficulties inherent in the original conception of the monument. Problems of construction mingle with aesthetic problems, although the forms are quite contrary to the usual ones.

While the chief difficulty in building the exteriors of great vaulted naves lies in supporting the roof and adjusting its weight to the thickness of the walls, in the Crypt, as a result of having gained space by hollowing out the age-old stability of the rock, the strain is not only from above but on the sides as well.

Its total length is 262 metres and its maximum height, across the transept, 41 metres. This space, starting from the entry, contains the vestibule, the atrium, a space between it and the great nave and the transept. Although each of these parts has its own scheme of decoration, there is unity of design in the whole.

The Hall, the Atrium and the space between are each 11 metres wide and their vaulting also rises to a height of 11 metres, the great nave reaching twice as high. The decoration is uniform in style. The Vestibule has four wide pilasters joined by Norman arches and vaulting with lunettes matching the side arches. The Atrium is more richly decorated, with pilasters, vaulting and Norman arches embossed with simple rustication. In the space between, whose vaulting is ribbed, are two great niches, where two huge archangels stand in attitudes of watchful meditation. They are the work of Carlos Ferreira. Their wings are uplifted, their arms rest on their swords, whose points are sunk into their plinths-Ten steps, the symbolic number in the Monument, lead down to the Screen.

The Screen.

The entrance to the great nave of the Crypt is through a wrought iron screen, the work of the artist José Espinós Alonso.

The architect who planned the Monument as a whole, designed the Screen, as well as all the other decoration. He must have realized the need to screen offthe great nave, and keeping to the Spanish tradition of wrought iron-work, conceived this excellent means of carrying out his plan.

The Screen is divided into three clearly-defined parts, separated by four gate posts, two against the side walls, the other two serving as jambs to the central gate. The four gateposts are decorated with figures of Holy Saints and Holy Heroes (1) in the order given below, starting from the top-left. This theme also predominates in the decoration of the Cupola. The iron-work is crested with angels at each side, with insignias of heroes and martyrs above the centre gateposts. The figure of St James tops the centre of the design crowned by the Cross and angels. The spaces between the posts are filled in by seven cross bars and eighteen vertical ones.

---

(1) The figures, which face the Vestibule and the High Altar, respectively, stand in the following order:

The Screen combines the elaborate detail of the Plateresque style with the modern treatment of its figures and ornaments. Polychrome is used, with restraint, to give lightness and transparency to the whole, an effect enhanced by the illumination of the Crypt.

FACING THE VESTIBULE

FIRST GATEPOST	SECOND GATEPOST	THIRD GATEPOST	FOURTH GATEPOST
St Mark	St Vicent	St Simon	St George
St Matthew	St Laurence	St Francis of Assis	St Gorgonio
St Luke	St Xaxier	St Milan	St Joan of Arc
St John	St Andrew	St Anthony the Abbot	St James
St John Chrysostom	St Cecily		St Francis of Borja

FACING THE HIGH ALTAR

St Anthony	St Edward	St Paul	St Domingo de Guzmán
St Frutos	St Louis	St Augustine	St Hermengild
St Francis of Paula	St Maurice	St Thomas	St Peter
St Domingo de la Calzada	St Ignatius	St John of the Cross	St Barbara
St Macarius	St Fernando	St Teresa	St Stephen

The Great Nave.

The great nave is divided into four sections, marked by series of wide arches with cross-vaulting that forms

panels showing the bare rock of the mountain in which
the Crypt lies. To right and left, six small chapels have
been hollowed in the walls of the nave surmounted by
large reliefs in alabaster. These illustrate scenes in the
life of the Virgin Mary related to the general meaning
and purpose of the Monument. To the right stand The
Immaculate Conception, Our Lady of Carmen and Our
Lady of Lorette, Patronesses of the Army and Navy and
Air Force respectively. The first two are the work of the
sculptor Carlos Ferraira. The third is by Ramón Mateu.
To the left, Our Lady of Africa, Our Lady of Mercy, Pa-
troness of Prisoners, and Our Lady of the Pillar, by
Ferreira, Lapayese and Matéu respectively.

The decoration of these Chapels is very restrained On
the Predellas of the altars are scenes from the life of the
Virgin in the form of tryptychs painted on leather, in the
style of the medieval Spanish portable altars of the Cru-
sades. Statues of the Apostles stand in niches on either
side. Paintings and sculpture are the work of the sculptor Lapayese and his son.

There is a certain primitive look about the whole Crypt,
which is neither forced nor mannered, but the result of
an unparallelled struggle to overcome technical difficulties without precedent in the history of architecture. It
was not a case of choosing one way out among many, but
of inventing or searching for a solution to entirely new
problems. Hence the air of simplicity and strength,
which faithfully reflects the nobility and high moral purpose of the builders' efforts.

The Tapestries of the Apocalypse.

The wall spaces of the great nave where the vaulted arches converge are decorated with eight magnificent pieces of tapestry forming the series illustrating the Apocalypse of St John.

These are woven in gold, silver, silk and wool, and are dated about 1540, judging from the clothes, architecture and style. They were woven by William Pannemaker of Brussels, whore mark appears on four of the panels, and they were bought by Philip II who brought them to Spain in 1553. The name of the fine artist who painted the cartoons for them has unfortunately never been discovered, although it seems clear that he must have been familiar with compositions on the same subject by Durero and Juan de Brujas. It is thought that they might be the work of Bernard Van Orley, who blended in the most brilliant, original way his own Flemish style with that of the Italian Renaissance, then beginning to make itself felt in the Low Countries.

The imaginative treatment of the various subjects, the skilful way in which so many elements are combined into one harmonious whole, the colour and texture of the threads, all go to make these tapestries one of the greatest universally known works of art. Many writers have called in the "Sistine Chapel of Northern Art". Each piece of tapestry measures 8.70 metres $\times$ 5.30, including their rich borders, no two alike.

The Apocalypse, a Greek word meaning revelation, contains St John the Baptist's revelation during his exile at Patmos. It is the only prophetic book in the New Testament, and the tapestry depicts each incident in the order in which they are described in the Book of St John. It also includes the apotheosis of the Lord, who looks down from Clouds of Glory upon the events taking place in piece of tapestry.

FIRST TAPESTRY.—The Revelations to St John made by seven angels, representing the seven churches of Asia, being in Patmos.

Scene I.— Two angels bear an inscription; behind them stands the Tree of Life. *Scene II.*— The Lord, enthroned on a double rainbow, holds out the Gospel upon his open left palm. On the right are seven stars; near his head is the two-edged flaming sword (the Divine Word); prostrated at his feet, St John receives the Revelations. This scene is framed with seven candelabra and bordered in clouds. *Scene III.* — St John, seated, receives the Revelations of the Angels, representing the Seven Churches of Asia, Ephesius, Smyrna, Philadelphia, Laodicea, Pergamo, Sardis and Tiatira, represented by fine speciments of architecture. *Scene IV.* — The angel, from one bank of the River of Life, shows St John, who kneels on the other, the apotheosis of the Lord, who, enthroned with the Lamb and the Book and flanked by the Tetramorphos, is encircled by 24 Elders, who offer up their golden crown, and the Seven Lamps. All this is bordered with clouds and stars.

SECOND TAPESTRY.—The Beginning of the Last Judgement.

Scene I.—The Four Horsemen of the Apocalypse. The three horsemen representing Famine, Plague and War, appear in the clouds accompanied bi the Symbols of the Evangelists; beneath them

Death, the fourth horseman, destroys humanity and behind him, Hell, in the form of a monster. The people clamour and hide in the hills. *Scene II.*—The Angel, bearing the Cross, the Symbol of the Redemption of Our Lord, commands·four others, placed at the four corners of the earth to subdue the winds, so that they shall do no harm. *Scene III.*—The angel points to the multitude of the Just, on their knees, bearing the Seal of God. *Scene IV.*—Angels, upon the Rainbow of the Lord, receive the Souls of the Just, represented by some nude figures, whom they clothe with celestial robes.

THIRD TAPESTRY.—The Destruction of Humanity by the Plagues, and the Worship of the Lamb.

Scene I.—The Lord delivers the trumpets to the Angels who announce the outbreak of the Plagues. Before the Altar of the Lord an angel stands ready to blow the first blast. *Scenes II and III.*—Representation of the Plagues. *Scene IV.*—St John, kneels in contemplation of the apotheosis of the Lamb, whose blood is received in a Chalice by a Pope.

FOURTH TAPESTRY.—The Story of Enoch and Elias.

Scene I.—St John receives the rod to measure the temple of the Lord. *Scene II.*—Enoch and Elias preach. *Scene III.*—Evil (a dragon) attacks both prophets, whose death is depicted is *Scene IV.* In *Scene V* the souls of the two prophets ascend into the Glory of the Lord, who receives them surrounded by 24 Elders. *Scene VI.*—The impious and the Dragon try to attack the Woman clothed in Sun (the Virgin), accompanied by an angel, who takes the new-born son, protected by the Lord, who appears on clouds near the Ark above the Rainbow. The destruction of Babylon appears in the background.

FIFTH TAPESTRY.—The Fight between Angels and Demons, who try to attack the Woman Clothed in Sun.

Scene I.—The Battle of St Michael and his angels with the infernal monsters. *Scenes II* and *III.*—The Virgin, Clothed in Sun, protected by the Angel who gives her eagle wings to fly to the desert from the seven-headed dragon. In *Scenes IV* and *V*, the Beast, emerging from the sea, is adored by the multitude, who raise altars to it and worship it on a pillar: another beast with ram's horns is also worshipped. *Scene VI.*—The Beast makes war on the Saints and the Faithful. *Scene VII.*—The Lamb and the Chosen on Mount Sion: in the background the waterfall representing the Songs of Praise. Christ surrounded by the 24 elders and the Symbols of the Evangelists preside over each scene.

SIXTH TAPESTRY.—The Triumph of the Gospel.

Scene I.—The angel shows the Gospel to the dwellers of earth. In *Scene II* the impious are tormented by flames and sulphur in front, of the angels and the Lamb. *Scenes III* and *IV.*—God the Son seated on a cloud above the rainbow, with a sickle in his right hand, orders the angel to punish the wicked. *Scenes V* and *VI.*—The symbol of St Mark, a human figure with a lion's head wearing a halo, gives the angels the order to throw the plagues in their cups on to the Earth.

SEVENTH TAPESTRY.

Scene I.—The Angels throw the contents of the cups of the Wrath of God over Babylon, the river Euphrates, and the Evil Beast; a group of merchants lament the ruin of Babylon. *Scene II.*—The whore (Babylon) sits at the water's edge with the king at her feet, drunk with the wine of their lust. *Scene III.*—The whore, mounted on the dragon with seven heads, offers the kings of the earth the cup of blood, symbol of abominations, and in the 4th scene she appears in flames, while her followers watch her torment: this scene is crowned by the Angel who cast the millstone into the sea. In *scenes V* and *VI,* God-the-Son, surrounded by the Tetramorphous and the Elders, celebrates the destruction of Babylon and the nuptials of the Lamb with the Church. *Scene VII.*—The Army of Christ follows the Saviour, enthroned with a Sceptre in one hand and the flaming two-edged sword in his mouth. *Scene VIII.*—The Angel, surmounting the Sun, calls the birds of the air to devour the carnal of the Earth.

EIGHTH TAPESTRY.—The Triumph of the Church over the Demon chained in Paradise.

Scene I.—The Army of Christ, mounted on white horses, fight the powers of Hell (the dragon with seven heads): they vanquish it and put it in chains in *Scene II.* In *Scene III,* the angel shows St John the Apotheosis of God-the-Son; the Holy City of Jerusalem appears under the protection of God-the-Father. The Church triumphant is represented by a walled city with towers: angels guard the doors and a group of the Just worship the preceding visions. In *Scene VI,* an angel bears an inscription, alluding to the series of tapestry panels.

Below the tapestries and sculptured frontispieces distinguishing each chapel, two rows of rustication run round the walls by way of frieze. These give solidity to what would otherwise look too fragile by counteracting the vertical lines with horizontal ones.

The Transept.

A flight of then steps leads from the great nave to the transept. Stout buttresses surmounted by sculpture representing the Army, Navy, Air Force and the Militias, divide and decorate this and are the work of Antonio Martín and Juan Antonio Sanguino. The rough carving of the uniforms contrasts with the polished treatment of the faces and hands.

In the central part of the transept the decorative schemes of the nave and the spaces preceding it are changed, yet harmony with them is achieved by this very means. The wall paintings are purely classical in style, and this classicism only varies in the four arches supporting the dome of the cupola, which are rusticated.

At the head of the transept stands the choir. Semicircular in shape, it is designed on three levels. It contains seventy choir-stalls, in classic style. There are two chapels, one on each side, with mosaic ceilings. That on the right forms the last Station of the Cross in the Via Crucis which encircles the Monument and runs round the Valley. On the altar of his Chapel there is a recumbent statue of Christ, carved in alabaster, with the figures of the Virgin and St John, one on either side. It is the work of Lapayese, and the serene majesty of the figure of our Lord is particularly impressive and belongs to the great tradition of Spanish polychrome sculpture in wood.

Right in the middle of the transept rising vertically in line with the giant Cross outside, stands the High Altar, hewn out of a mighty monolith of polished granite. The front of the Predella is decorated with a bas-relief of the Burial of Christ, in gilt, designed by the architect Diego Méndez and carved by Espinós. The back of the Predella represents the Last Supper.

The only sculpture on the altar is a monumental figure carved in wood of Christ Crucified, the work of the Sculptor Beovide, a pupil of the famous painter Ignacio Zuloaga, who polychromed the carving.

The figure of Christ, with its three nails, is a very fine piece of work. Notwithstanding the anatomical detail of the torso and abdomen, the forms are rounded and the legs long and sturdy. There is no writhing tortured expression of pain; the serene face is entirely uncovered, and the tranquillity of the whole composition enhances the majesty of the Saviour.

The Cupola.

The mosaics of the Cupola ceiling crown the whole Transept. The art of mosaics was inherited by Spain from Rome, and widely practised. Spanish museums and private collections contain magnificent specimens of murals and paving; but the use of mosaics to decorate the ceiling of a Cupola is an innovation made for the first time in the Valley of the Fallen. The richness and complex nature of the composition recall the variety characteristic of Italian mosaics. It is Byzantine in style, although strongly influenced by medieval Spanish illuminated Codex without losing sight of modern realistic tendencies.

The dome is a blaze of colour, owing to the variety and purity of each *Tessela* of the mosaic. It thus makes the necessary contrast with the stony severity of the murals in the Transept. It even gives the illusion of a retable to the High Altar, which it covers and seems to support.

As to the subject, Christ seated encircled by angels, a modern conception of the *Pantocrator,* forms the centre of groups of Saints, heroes and martyrs, doctors, Popes, prelates and peasants on their way to the glory of the Lord. The image of the Virgin forms another centre to the processions making their way towards the throne of God. It is the work of Santiago Padrós, and the clever grouping gives an effect of great space and height to the dome.

The necessary adjuncts to the church, such as passages leading to the lift in the dome and the interior of the Cross, and to the rear portico, complete this great subterranean Basilica, whose dimensions make it the largest ever built in the history of mankind.

The Centre of Social Studies.

As an integral part of the Foundation of the Holy Cross of the Valley of the civil war Deads, and together with the religious aim of the monument, the Spanish head of State Francisco Franco Bahamonde — patron to the society — established another equally fundamental aim: the creation of a Centre of Social Studies in order to work upon the knowledge and implantation of peace amongst men based upon Christian social justice.

It is situated in extensive areas purposely set up for

this organisation in the surrondings of the most beautiful stoop of the Abbey on its northern side.

The original by-laws for the development of this objective are based upon the following points—:

To pursue the up-to-date evolution of social thought in the world, its legislation and manifestation.

To compile the doctrine of both the Popes and catholic thinkers upon the subject.

To maintain an up-to-date library of religious and social catholic material and to execute all editing and in turn publish those works upon the social material carried on in the Centre.

To prepare that work or information concerning social problems commissioned by the directors.

In the year 1961 the task of the Centre was initiated which was divided into six sections: Morality and Social systems, file of the social doctrine of the Popes and social achievements, the social structure of Spain, sociology of the economic development, courses and publications, and libraries.

The job of the organisation of courses selection of work-crews for investigation, preparation of the filing index of the social doctrine and acquisition of funds for the library was began in June 1961. In the same year was started the publication of the Centre of Social Studies' bulletin, which is in its 4th year and comprises of 12 volumes. As a result of this work and profitable investigations a publication of a collection of Annals compiled in monographic volumes was began in 1962, concerning all studies carried out in the Centre.

The Centre has organised and patronised various enquiries and investigatory works upon social structure problems, co-operative organisation, emigration and consumer standards in Spain. This type of work has allowed it to co-operate effectively in the "Ponencia" of social assumptions of the plan of the Spanish Social Economic Development established in 1964. Besides, during the 3 years of its existence an index filing system has been completed concerning social doctrine. It is open to the public with a total of 13.200 cards in both Spanish and original tongue which will serve as a ground for the preparation of volumes that will give the maximum amount of diffusion to this wealth of social catholic thought.

The Centre organises courses in order to complete the social formation of University students and for those who hold a responsability of management in Spanish co-operatives. These courses have been organised with a cyclical and systematic character and form a basis for the issuing of a diploma. They have expanded beyond their own site in the Valley in order to set up branches in other regions of Spain directed by the Centre. In the year 1965 the extension of the Seminar of Pedagogic and Social Didactic will mean the organisation of special courses for Secondary and Primary school-teachers.

The Social Institute Leon XIII under the patronisation of the Centre organises intensive summer courses within the isolation and the use of boarding facilities of the sites situated in the Valley. That way enables many sudents — especially priests — to follow similar courses to those of the Social Institute Leon XIII in Madrid —which has recently been set up as a faculty of University by the Holy See. There are also courses of social formation, patronised by the Syndical Organisation.

One of the most important types of work carried out by the Centre has been the meeting of investigatory teams which edit and prepare their essays upon a central theme of study and discuss them at the Round Table in order to outline a doctrine upon the proposed question.

At these meetings of the Round Table, foreign professors are invited who compare their points of view with Spanish specialists and their surverys. Afterwards those matters are reviewed by a public discussion and so come to the light in the volumes of the Annals above mentioned.

The published titles up to present date are as follows— :

I.   From the Rerum Novarum to the Mater et Magistra.

II.   Man and Economy.

III. The artisan and co-operative company as regards to the catholic social doctrine.

IV.   Moral problems of the Company in relation to work.

V.   Science, investigation and technics in the presence of economic development and social progress.

VI.   The co-operativism in present day opportunities in Spain.

VII. Moral problems of the Company in relation to the State.

VIII. Social, economic and moral problems of the movement of the Spanish population.

IX.   Spanish agriculture, co-operativism and other forms of agrarian association.

X.   Moral problems of the Company in relation to society.

This mere annunciation will give an idea of the importance of the work carried out.

The Library subscribes to the most important reviews, and already has a collection up to present day of some 10.000 volumes. Those who may like to work on it may consult the duplicated files which are in Madrid, attached to the Balmes Institute Library, Medinaceli street, number 4, 4th floor.

Lonja, Monastery and Hostel.

Along the opposite side to the entrance to the Monument runs a series of buildings that are quite a monument in themselves. They consist of a Cloister, a back gate, a Monastery and a Noviciate, on one side, and of a Hostel and Study Centre on the other, and they conform to the gigantic scale the Valley demands. They are all built of granite with slate roofs. Enclosed by a fine arcade of columns and Norman arches, they occupy a rectangular space of 300 metres by 150.

From this group of buildings the, great size of the monumental Cross adds to the beauty and majesty of the Monument, uniting its architecture, sculpture and decorative arts in one harmonious whole.

Without any sense of rivalry, it conforms to the severe, ascetic mould in which it was conceived, and it takes its place among the great, architectural and artistic creations of all time.

Entrada al Valle
Entrée au "Valle"
"Valles's" entrance

Talseingang
Entrata al "Valle"
Entrada ao "Valle"

Los Juanelos
Les "Juanelos"
The "Juanelos"

Die "Juanelos"
"Los Juanelos"
Os "Juanelos"

Vista general   Gesamtansicht
Vue générale   Vista generale
General view   Vista geral

Vista general   Gesamtansicht
Vue générale   Vista generale
General view   Vista geral

Vista de la Cruz y Jardines
Vue de la Croix et Jardins
View of the Cross and Gardens

Kreuz und Gärten
Vista della Croce e Giardini
Vista da Cruz e Jardins

Vista de la Cruz y Jardines
Vue de la Croix et Jardins
View of the Cross and Gardens

Kreuz und Gärten
Vista della Croce e Giardini
Vista da Cruz e Jardins

Vista de la Cruz y Jardines
Vue de la Croix et Jardins
View of the Cross and Gardens

Kreuz und Gärten
Vista della Croce e Giardini
Vista da Cruz e Jardins

Vista de la Cruz y aparcamientos   Kreuz und parkanlagen
Vue de la Croix et parking   Vista della Croce e ''parking''
View of the Cross and parking   Vista da Cruz e o estacionamento

Fachada principal del Monumento
Façade principale du Monument
Main façade of the Monument

Hauptansicht der Vorderseite des Monumentes
Facciata principale del Monumento
Fachada principal do Monumento

Vista frontal de la Cruz (alt. 150 m.)   Vorderansicht des Kreuzes
Vue frontale de la Croix   Vista frontale della Croce
Frontal view of the Cross   Vista frontal da Cruz

La Piedad   Die Pietät
La Pieté   La Pieta
The Pity   A Piedade

Puerta de entrada a la Basílica   Eintrittstür der Basilika
Porte d´entrée a la Basilique   Porta di entrata alla Basilica
Entrance gate to the Basilica   Porta de entrada da Basílica

Cripta-Basílica. Reja   Gruft-Basilika. Gitter
Crypte-Basilique. Grille   Cripta-Basilica. Inferriata
Crypt-Church. Grate   Cripta-Basilica. Grade

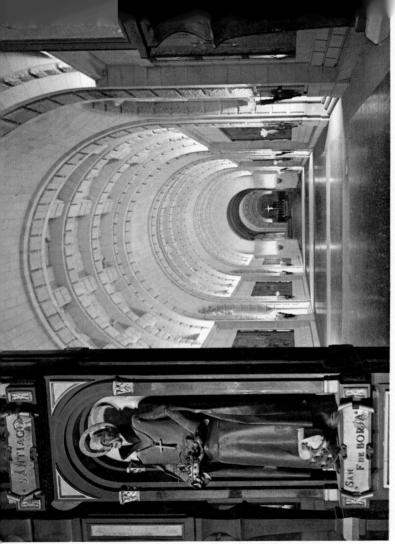

Cripta Basílica. Detalle
Crypte-Basilique. Détail
Crypt-Church. Detail

Gruft-Basilika. Detail
Cripta-Basilica. Dettaglio
Cripta-Basilica . Pormenor

Virgen del Pilar   Hl. Jungfrau Pilar
Vierge du Pilar   Vergine del Pilar
Virgin of the Pilar   Virgen do Pilar

Cripta-Basílica. Nave central
Crypte-Basilique. Nef centrale
Crypt-Church. Central nave

Gruft-Basilika. Mittelschiff
Cripta-Basilica. Navata centrale
Cripta-Basilica . Nave central

Virgen de Africa   Hl. Jungfrau Africa
Vierge d´Africa   Vergine di Africa
Virgin of Africa   Virgen de Africa

Virgen de Loreto   Hl. Jungfrau Loreto
Vierge de Loreto   Vergine di Loreto
Virgin of Loreto   Virgen de Loreto

Virgen del Carmen   Hl. Jungfrau Carmen
Vierge du Carmen   Vergine del Carmen
Virgin of the Carmen   Virgen do Carmen

Altar de la Virgen de la Merced   Altar der hl. Jungfrau Merced
Autel de la Vierge de la Merced   Altare della Vergine della Mercede
Altar of the Virgin of the Merced   Altar de Virgen de Mercê

Cripta-Basílica   Gruft-Basilika
Crypte-Basilique   Cripta-Basilica
Crypt-Church   Cripta-Basilica

Tapiz del Apocalipsis de San Juan
Tapis de l'Apocalipsis de St. Jean
"Apocalipsis de San Juan" Tapestry

Apokalipse teppich von Heilig Johann
Tappeto dell'Apocalipsis
Tapiz do Apocalipse de São João

QVIS SIMILIS BESTIE ET QVIS POTERIT PVGNARE CVM E

Tapiz del Apocalipsis de San Juan
Tapis de l'Apocalipsis de St. Jean
"Apocalipsis de San Juan" Tapestry

Apokalipse teppich von Heilig Johann
Tappeto dell'Apocalipsis
Tapiz do Apocalipse de São João

Tapiz del Apocalipsis de San Juan
Tapis de l' Apocalipsis de St. Jean
"Apocalipsis de San Juan" Tapestry

Apokalipse teppich von Heilig Johann
Tappeto dell' Apocalipsis
Tapiz do Apocalipse de São João

Cripta-Basílica. Altar Mayor
Crypte-Basilique. Maître-Autel
Crypt-Church. Main Altar

Gruft-Basilika. Hautaltar
Cripta-Basilica. Altare Maggiore
Cripta-Basilica. Altar Maior

Detalle del Altar Mayor
Détail du Maître-Autel
Detail of the Main Altar

Detail des Hauptaltars
Dettaglio dell'Altare Maggiore
Pormenor do Altar Maior

AZRAEL. Escultura en bronce (alt. 8 m.)   Bronzeskulptur
Sculpture en bronze   Scultura di bronzo
Sculpture in bronze   Escultura em bronze

El Arcángel S. Miguel. Escultura en bronce (alt. 8 m.)
Sitial del Jefe del Estado
Siège du Chef d'Etat
Presiding chair of the, Head of the State

Ehrensitzt Staatschef
Seggio del Capo di Stato
Setial do Chefe do Estado

El Arcángel S. Gabriel. Escultura en bronce (alt. 8 m.)

Sitial del Padre Abad	Ehrensitzt vom Abt Pater
Siège du Père Abbé	Seggio del Padre Abate
Presiding chair of the Father Abbot	Setial do Padre Abade

El Arcángel San Rafael.
Escultura en bronce (alt. 8 m.)
Sculpture en bronze
Sculpture in bronze

Bronzeskulptur
Scultura di bronzo
Escultura em bronze

Cripta-Basílica. Altar Mayor
Crypte-Basilique. Maître-Autel
Crypt-Church. Main Altar

Gruft-Basilika. Hautaltar
Cripta-Basilica. Altare Maggiore
Cripta-Basilica . Altar Maior

Basílica. Detalle del Altar Mayor
Basilique. Détail du Maître-Autel
Church. Detail of the Main Altar

Basilika. Detail des Hauptaltars
Basilica. Dettaglio dell'Altare Maggiore
Basilica. Pormenor do Altar Maior

Cristo del Altar Mayor
Christ du Maître-Autel
Christ of the Main Altar

Christur von Hochaltar
Cristo dell´Altare Maggiore
Cristo do Altar Maior

Cripta de la Basílica. Mosaico de la bóveda
Crypte de la Basilique. Mosaique de la voûte
Crypt of the Basilica. Mosaic of the vault

Gruft der Basilika. Mosaik des Gewölbes
Cripta della Basilica. Mosaico della volta
Cripta da Basilica. Mosaico de abóbeda

Cripta-Basílica. Cristo y bóveda
Crypte-Basilique. Christ et voûte
Crypt-Church. Christ and vault

Gruft-Basilika. Christus und Gewölbe
Cripta della Basilica. Cristo e volta
Cripta-Basilica. Cristo e Abóbeda

Altar desde el Coro

Coro   Chor
Chœur   Coro
Choir   Coro

Escolanía en el coro
Manécanterie dans le chœur
Singing boys in the choir

Chorsänger im Chor
Coro della scolaresca
Escolania no coro

Altar del Santísimo   Heligsteraltar
Autel du "Santísimo"   Altare del Santissimo
"Santísimo´s" Altar   Altar do Santíssimo

Altar fin del Via Crucis
Autel fin du Via Crucis
Altar at the end of the Via Crucis

Altar der Kreuzigung
Altare fine delle Via Crucis
Altar fim do Via Crucis

Vista panorámica de la parte posterior del Monumento   Panorama der Rückseite des Monumentes
Vue panoramique de la part postérieure du Monument   Veduta panoramica della parte posteriore del Monumen
Panoramic view of the back of the Monument   Vista panorâmica da parte posterior do Monumento

Salida de la parte posterior   Hinterer Ausgang
Sortie de la partie postérieure   Uscita della parte posteriore
Sally of the posterior part   Saída da parte posterior

La Cruz   Das Kreuz
La Croix   La Croce
The Cross   A Cruz

Vista de la Cruz (alt. 150 m.)   Ansicht des Kreuzes
Vue de la Croix   Vista della Croce
View of the Cross   Vista da Cruz

Figura de San Mateo   Figur des St. Matthäus
Figure de Saint Mathieu   Figura di S. Matteo
St. Mattew´s figure   Figura de São Mateus

Detalle parte posterior con el Convento y Seminario
Détail part postérieure avec le Couvent et Seminaire
Detail back-side with the Convent and Seminary

Teil der Rückseite mit Kloster und Seminar
Dettaglio della parte posteriore, Convento e Seminario
Pormenor parte posterior com o Convento e Seminário

Figura de San Lucas   Heilig Lukas
Figure de Saint Luc   Figura di San Luca
St. Luke´s figure   Figura de São Lucas

Figura de San Marcos   Heilig Markos
Figure de Saint Marc   Figura di San Marco
St. Mark´s figure   Figura de São Marcos

San Juan Evangelista (alt. 18 m.)
Saint Jean Evangéliste
St. John Evangelist

St. Johannes Evangelist
S. Giovanni Evangelista
São Yoão Evangelista

Vista panorámica de la parte posterior del Monumento
Vue panoramique de la part postérieure du Monument
Panoramic view of the back of the Monument

Panorama der Rückseite des Monumentes
Veduta panoramica della parte posteriore del Monumento
Vista panorâmica da parte posterior do Monumento

La Cruz (alt. 150 m.) desde el estanque

Das Kreuz. Sicht vom Teich

La Croix dès l'étang

La Croce. Dallago

The Cross from the pond

A Cruz desde o lago artificial

Panorámica   Panorama
Panoramique   Panorama
Panoramic   Panorâmica

Poblado del Valle   Talsansicht
Vue du "Valle"   Vista della "Valle"
"Valle's" view   Vista do "Valle"

Vista panorámica de la parte posterior del Monumento
Vue panoramique de la parte postérieure du Monument
Panoramic view of the back of the Monument
Panorama der Rückseite des Monumentes
Veduta panoramica della parte posteriore del Monumento
Vista panorâmica da parte posterior do Monumento

Vista panorámica   Panorama
Vue panoramique   Panorama
Panoramic view   Vista panorâmica

Entrada al funicular
Entrée au funiculaire
Entrance to the funicular

Eingang zur Seilbahn
Accesso al funiculare
Entrada al funicular

Vista del Monumento desde el Via Crucis
Vue du Monument dès "Via Crucis"
View of the Monument from "Via Crucis"

Denkmal von Via Crucis aus
Vista del Monumento da il "Via Crucis"
Vista do Monumento desde o "Via Crucis"

La Cruz (alt. 150 m.) desde el Via Crucis
La Croix dès "Via Crucis"
The Cross from "Via Crucis"

Das Kreuz gesehen von der "Via Crucis"
La Croce dalla "Via Crucis"
A Cruz desde a "Via Crucis"

Estación en el Via Crucis   Station in dem "Via Crucis"
Station du "Via Crucis"   Stazione nel "Via Crucis"
Station in the "Via Crucis"   Estação no "Via Crucis"

Camino del Via Crucis
Chemin du "Via Crucis"
"Via Crucis" way

Weg zum "Via Crucis"
Cammino del "Via Crucis"
Caminho do "Via Crucis"

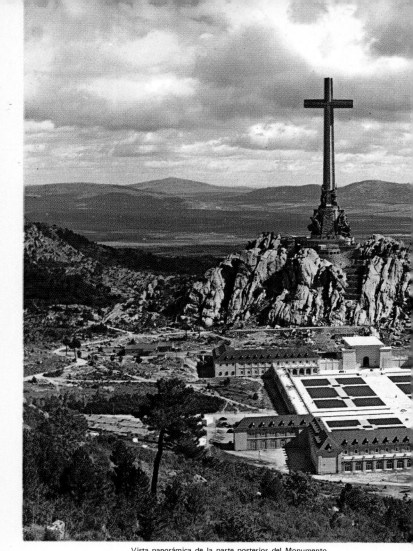

Vista panorámica de la parte posterior del Monumento
Vue panoramique de la part postérieure du Monument
Panoramic view of the back of the Monument

Panorama der Rückseite des Monumentes
Veduta panoramica della parte posteriore del Monumento
Vista panorâmica da parte posterior do Monumento

Claustro del Centro de Estudios Sociales
Cloître du Centre d´Etudes Sociaux
Cloister of the Centre of Social Studies

Kreuzgang der Unterrichtsanstalt von sozial Studium
Claustro del Centro degli Studi Sociali
Claustro de Centro de Estudios Sociais

La Cruz   Das Kreuz
La Croix   La Croce
The Cross   A Cruz

TOURISTICAL GUIDES

PATRIMONIO NACIONAL

Madrid. *Royal Orient Palace.*
Madrid. *Royal Armoury.*
Madrid. *Museum of Carriages.*
Madrid. *Monasteries-Museums of the Royal Descalzas and the Church of the Incarnation.*
Madrid. *Moncloa Palace.*
El Pardo (Palace-Museum, House of the Prince and Palace of La Quinta).
Palace-Monastery with the Houses of the Prince and of Arriba at San Lorenzo of El Escorial.
National Monument of Santa Cruz of the Valle de los Caídos.
Aranjuez: *History, Palaces-Museums and Gardens.*
Royal Palace of La Granja and Palace-Residence with the Hunting Museum, in Riofrío. Segovia.
Museum-Monastery of the Huelgas and the Palace of the Isla, in Burgos, *and the Museum-Monastery of Santa Clara at Tordesillas.* Valladolid.
Seville's Royal Alcázares.
Barcelona. *Palace of Pedralbes and Albéniz Small Palace.*

LIBRERIA DEL PATRIMONIO NACIONAL
Plaza de Oriente, 6 (esquina a Felipe V) — Madrid-13

SEGOVIA

RIOFRIO

LA GRANJA

86 Km.

a Avila

San Rafael

Puerto de Navacerrada

MONUMENTO
NACIONAL A
LOS CAIDOS

Guadarrama

Villalba

64 Km.

ESCORIAL

EL PARDO

45 Km.

Las Rozas

MADRID

a Toledo   70 Km.

47 Km.

ARANJUEZ